WRITING SKILLS

Written by **Christine Hood**

Illustrated by **Dave Garbot**

FlashKids™

A division of Spark Publishing
NEW YORK

This book belongs to

_____

Executive Editor: Hanna Otero
Managing Editor: Vincent Janoski
Graphic Designer: April Ward
Editor: Eliza Berkowitz

This edition published by Spark Publishing

Spark Publishing
A Division of SparkNotes LLC
120 Fifth Avenue, 8th Floor
New York, NY 10011

ISBN 1-4114-0023-2

Please send all comments and questions or
report errors to www.sparknotes.com/errors

Printed in China

Dear Parent,

Good reading and writing skills are essential to your child's success in school. The activities in this book are designed to help your child get excited about writing. Through a variety of engaging writing exercises, your child will learn how to put words together to write purposefully and creatively. The activities are meant to inspire your child to write using different genres, such as poetry, persuasion, newspaper articles, facts and opinions, description, comparison, and more. The last few pages of the book provide several story organizing charts. Use these charts to help your child organize his or her ideas before writing. To encourage your child to read and write on a daily basis, try some of the following suggestions:

- Be a role model for your child. Read and write often as part of your daily routine.
- Invite your child to help you with shopping and "to-do" lists.
- Have your child start a daily journal. Let him or her know that the journal is a place to write about personal thoughts and feelings.
- Involve your child in writing important dates on the family calendar, such as special events, birthdays, anniversaries, and holidays.
- Encourage your child to write letters and postcards to friends and relatives.
- Offer lots of praise and support.
- Let your child reward his or her work with the included stickers.
- Create a special place in the house where you and your child can read every day!

Sensory Words

Sensory words tell how someone or something looks, sounds, smells, feels, or tastes. Good writers use sensory words to make their writing more interesting. Write **look**, **sound**, **smell**, **feel**, or **taste** after each sentence to tell which sense is being used.

1. Jesse was cold and wet when he climbed out of the pool. *feel*

2. The tires squealed loudly as the car rounded the corner. *sound*

3. Mia's little white dog had curly hair and a fat, bushy tail. *look*

4. The grass smelled fresh and clean after the rain. *smell*

5. The sour lemons added the perfect touch to the sweet lemonade. *taste*

6. The soup was too spicy for her liking. *taste*

7. The kitten felt soft and warm in her arms. *feel*

8. Bryan yelled so loud they had to cover their ears. *sound*

Write with Your Senses

Write a sentence for each topic below using sensory words. Remember to think of your five senses: sight, hearing, touch, smell, and taste.

1. fresh apple pie

   Fresh apple pie tastes good.

2. crying baby

   I hear the crying baby.

3. small puppy

   The small puppy touch like a Pillow.

4. bright sun

   Todays has a bright sun.

5. ocean breeze

   Ocean breeze feels good.

6. new car

   My mom was happy to get her new car.

7. baking bread

   the cheef was baking bread and it smells good.

Body Talk

Think of all the different things you can do with your body. Sure, you can sit, walk, and jump. But what else can you do? Use the code below to find more interesting words you can use in your writing. To "crack the code," write the letter that comes before each one shown on the lines.

Yawnnnn

A	B	C	D	E	F	G	H	I	J	K	L	M
N	O	P	Q	R	S	T	U	V	W	X	Y	Z

1. D S F F Q   C R E E P

2. C P V O D F   B o u n c e

3. U V N C M F   T u m b l e

4. T M P V D I   S L O U C H

5. T R V J O U   S Q U I N T

6. H S B T Q   G R A S P

7. Q S P X M   P R O W L

8. T U S V U   S t r u t

Now, choose three words from above and use each in a sentence.

You are a creep.

I can bounce higher than you

Exciting Emotions

We all know words like happy and sad, but there are many more interesting words you can use to describe your feelings! Unscramble each word below, and then write it in the sentence it fits best.

PEHOFUL — _hopeful_

LFUBTDOU — _Doutbful_

EDBOR — _Bored_

OUDPR — _Proud_

ELYLON — _Lonely_

DEKSHCO — _Shocked_

Dead Bug

1. Josh was _hopeful_ that his favorite team would win.

2. Lin was _bored_ by the dead bug.

3. The whole class was _proud_ of their first-place award.

4. I didn't study for the test. It is _Doutbful_ I will get

a good grade.

5. After her friend moved away, Maya felt _lonely_.

6. Kayley was _Bored_ with softball and wanted to

try a new sport.

Think of another word for:

sad: _lonely_   happy: _proud_

tired: _Bored_   scared: _frintim_

On another sheet of paper, use each new word in a sentence.

7

Describing Words

Describing words tell about a person, place, animal, or thing. Some describing words are more interesting than others. For example, **gigantic** is more interesting than **big**. Write interesting describing words to complete the paragraph below.

I'll never forget when I first saw my dog, Brandy. I found her at the county shelter. She was in a cage with some other dogs, but her _____big_____ bark got my attention. Her entire body wriggled with _____sadness_____! She seemed so _____sad_____ that I asked if I could take her for a walk. It was a _____beautiful_____ day as Brandy and I took our first walk together. I scratched the _____Black_____ fur behind her _____furry_____ ears, and she licked me with her _____pink_____ tongue. I knew we would be _____best_____ friends!

On another piece of paper, write what happened next in the story. Make sure to use interesting words!

Description Cube

Write a descriptive paragraph about your favorite food, movie, book, animal, sport, or other activity. Remember, descriptions should use interesting words to help the reader see, smell, feel, taste, hear, and even understand an object.

Fill in this Description Cube to help you organize your ideas for your paragraph. Then write your paragraph on another piece of paper. Use your cube to help you.

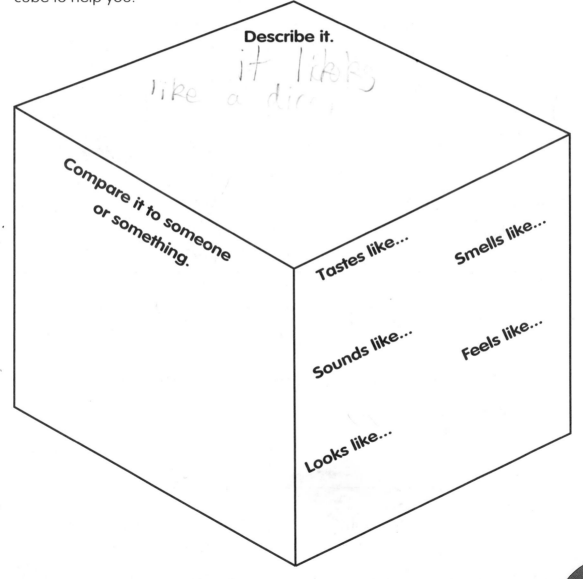

Describe it.

it liks like a dic

Compare it to someone or something.

Tastes like...

Smells like...

Sounds like...

Feels like...

Looks like...

Synonym Search

Synonyms are words with the same or similar meanings. **Happy** and **joyful** are synonyms. The words in the box are synonyms for the words in bold in the story below. Rewrite the story using the synonym for each word in bold. Read your new paragraph aloud.

delicious	astonished	raced	grinned	shouted	present
excitedly	finest	quickly	gobbled	bounced	begins

Jamie woke up and **smiled**. Today was his birthday! He **jumped** out of bed and **ran** to the kitchen. His mom was baking him a **tasty** chocolate cake. "You better get ready," Mom said. "Your party **starts** in one hour." "I can't wait!" Jamie **said joyfully**. He **ate** his breakfast **fast**, and then went to get dressed in his **best** clothes. Little did Jamie know the special **gift** that was waiting for him. He was **surprised**!

_____

_____

_____

_____

_____

_____

On another piece of paper, write what happened next in the story. What was Jamie's big surprise? Make sure to use interesting words!

Hurray for Homophones!

Homophones are words that sound the same but have different meanings and spellings. For example, **hear** and **here** are homophones. Choose the correct homophone to complete each sentence below.

1. Jennifer was finally able to _meet_ her pen pal. (meet, meat)

2. I bought a _pair_ of shoes and a skirt at the mall. (pear, pair)

3. The flower garden gave off a wonderful _scent_. (cent, scent)

4. The strong wind _blew_ the door open. (blew, blue)

5. We looked through the _mail_ to find their letter. (mail, male)

6. My favorite fairy _tale_ is *Twelve Dancing Princesses*. (tail, tale)

On another piece of paper, write sentences using three of the homophone pairs below.

bee/be   toe/tow   wear/where   road/rode   right/write   sea/see

Lovely Alliteration

A beginning letter sound repeated in a sentence is called **alliteration**. Here is an example: **Seven snoring snakes snoozed in the sun**. Use alliteration to write silly sentences with the words below. Add more words that begin with the same sound to complete your sentences.

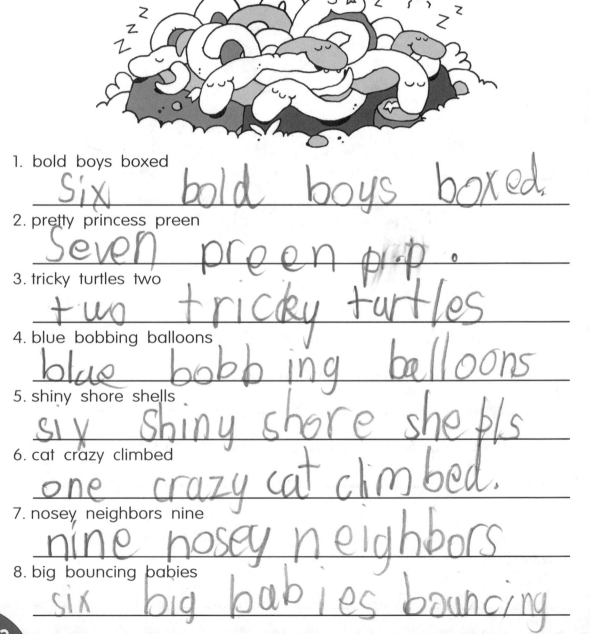

1. bold boys boxed

   Six bold boys boxed.

2. pretty princess preen

   Seven preen prp.

3. tricky turtles two

   two tricky turtles

4. blue bobbing balloons

   blue bobbing balloons

5. shiny shore shells

   six shiny shore shells

6. cat crazy climbed

   one crazy cat climbed.

7. nosey neighbors nine

   nine nosey neighbors

8. big bouncing babies

   six big babies bouncing

Alliteration Poem

Remember, **alliteration** is a beginning letter sound repeated in a sentence. Read the alliteration poem below.

Brandy's baking bread,

While Nolan nibbles nuts.

Corey climbs and cartwheels,

While Lisa leaps in loops.

Trey is tickling Trixie,

While Sam is swinging Steph.

Dave is drawing dinosaurs,

While Paula pats her pet.

My friends and I have so much fun,

I wouldn't trade them for anyone!

Now, write your own alliteration poem using the names of your friends and family. Write their names first, and then list words that begin with the same letter sound. Then write your poem below. Draw a frame around your poem.

_____

_____

_____

_____

_____

_____

Rhyming Words

Rhyming words end with the same sound. For example, **dish** and **fish** rhyme, and so do **wake** and **break**. In each row, circle the word that rhymes with the first.

1. **bright**:   bat   stair   (bite)   mall   tide
2. **tale**:   love   (mail)   milk   tame   school
3. **tend**:   ham   brake   pen   stone   (mend)
4. **think**:   tile   (sink)   him   share   math

Now think of a good rhyming word to complete each rhyme below.

5. I love the stars, they shine so **bright**,

   They twinkle with a glowing

   _sight_____

6. It's like a garden you need to **ten**

   To be a good and caring

   _mend_____

7. I'm no fish, but I have fins and a **tail**,

   What am I? I'm a big blue

   _ball_____

8. If I mix up red and white, I **think**,

   The color that I'll see is

   _Black ink_____

Rhyme Time

Rhyming words end with the same sound. Think of a good rhyming word to complete each rhyme below.

1. The little oozy, slimy **snail**,

   Crawled and left a gooey

   snob

2. The nervous mouse began to **speak**,

   But all we heard was a tiny

   squeak

3. At first my nose began to **wheeze**,

   And then exploded with a giant

   sneeze

4. I love cookies, cakes, and **pies**,

   I love

   nies

Now write your own poem:

I love *dogs*

I love *cats*

Hink Pinks

Hink Pinks are riddles that "play" with words. The answers are rhyming word pairs.

Example:

What is an overweight feline?

A fat cat!

Write the answer to each Hink Pink below by unscrambling the words.
Remember, the words rhyme!

1. What is an "undressed" seat?   EARB   IRHCA

   A Bear on a chair

2. What is a strong blossom?   ERWOP   FEOLWR

   A Power Flower

3. What is an unhappy father?   DSA   ADD

   A sad dad

4. What is a journey by boat?   IHSP   PRTI

   A Ship Trip

5. What is pretty money?   TEUC   OTOL

   A cute Tool

6. What is a nice road?   WTEES   STTEER

   A sweet street

7. What is the finest bird's home?   ETSB   TNSE

   A Best nest

Write two of your own Hink Pinks on another piece of paper.

Complete Sentences

A sentence should contain a complete thought.

A sentence without a complete thought is an incomplete sentence.

Incomplete sentence:

Jose's two friends

Complete sentence:

Jose's two friends play baseball.

Write **C** next to each complete sentence and **I** next to each incomplete sentence. If the sentence is complete, add a period to the end of the sentence. If the sentence is incomplete, write a complete sentence on the line below it.

1. ___I___ In the next class

_____

2. ___I___ Loved to go ice skating

_____

3. ___C___ We bought a new blue couch

_____

4. ___I___ In Joey's backyard

_____

5. ___C___ Shelly is a good swimmer

_____

6. ___C___ Three kittens played on the rug

_____

7. ___I___ On her spelling test

_____

8. ___I___ Mia's best friend

_____

Match It!

Match each sentence beginning with its ending to make a complete sentence.

We have been best friends

Brenda is better at math

We can't meet you tonight

Molly's new bike

Ms. Gonzales was upset

It isn't windy enough

Caitlyn is the best swimmer

than reading.

to fly a kite.

for five years.

on the swim team.

because we have too much homework.

about her lost dog.

is shiny and red.

Combining Sentences

Writers often put short sentences together into longer sentences so their writing doesn't sound choppy. You can join sentences using words such as **and, or, but**, or **so**.

Short sentences: Treana likes pizza. She likes spaghetti better.

Combined sentence: Treana likes pizza but she likes spaghetti better.

Join each pair of sentences together to make one longer sentence.

1. I like to read. I love to write.

    I like to read and I love to write.

2. The cat climbed the tree. I couldn't get her down.

    The cat climbed the tree but I couldn't get her down.

3. I was hungry. I decided to make a sandwich.

    I was hungry so I decided to make a sandwich.

4. I could go to the mall. I could go to the museum.

    I could go to the mall and I could go to the museum.

5. Sean is a good athlete. He is a talented singer.

    Sean is a good athlete and He is a talented singer.

6. The puppies were tired. They slept in the basket.

    The puppies were tired so they slept in the basket.

7. We turned on the heater. It made us warm.

    We turned on the heater so it made us warm.

 # Fix It!

Read the paragraph below. Some sentences are incomplete. Circle the incomplete sentences. Then rewrite the paragraph on the lines below using only complete sentences.

The Incredible Starfish

Did you know that starfish aren't really fish? That's why some people call them sea stars! Have five arms, like a star, but some have up to twelve A starfish has. Hundreds of tiny suckers on the bottom of each arm. These suckers help it move and eat. If one of its arms breaks off. It can grow a whole new arm. The arm can even grow into a whole new starfish!

_____

_____

_____

_____

_____

_____

_____

Better Sentences

Another way writers create good sentences is to combine two or more sentences that repeat the same words or ideas.

Example:

Dogs are great pets. Cats are great pets.

Dogs and cats are great pets.

Combine the sentences below by adding **and, or, but**, or **so**. Cross out words you want to take out. Write your new sentence below.

1. Jessica loves to skate. Jessica loves to dance.

   Jessica loves to skate and dance.

2. We could see a movie. We could go to the park.

   We could see a movie a. g. t. t. p.

3. The coats were expensive. The shoes were expensive.

   The coats and shoes w. e.

4. I would love to visit Alaska. I would also like to visit Brazil.

   I woould love to V. Al. A. Br.

5. We could plant a garden. We could sell the vegetables.

   We could plant a garden a. s. t. v.

6. Science is my favorite subject. Spanish is my other favorite subject.

   Science and spanish i. m. f. s.

7. We can paint the house yellow. We can paint the house white.

   We cand painit the h. y. o. w.

8. Is the earth round? Is the earth flat?

   Is the earth round or flat.

The Perfect Paragraph

A **paragraph** is a group of sentences that has one main idea. The main idea is supported by details that tell about the idea. Write the main idea of each paragraph below.

Did you know that spiders have eight eyes? Did you know that a spider's web can be stronger than steel? Did you know that spiders aren't insects? These are only a few amazing facts about these arachnids. Spiders are very interesting creatures!

Did you know that spiders have eight eyes.

The queen bee is the leader of a hive. She is actually the mother of all the other bees in the colony, which can be as many as 50,000! Queen bees can live anywhere from two to five years. In her short lifetime, a queen bee may lay as many as one million eggs.

The queen bee is the leader of the hive.

Supporting Details

Remember, a paragraph has one main idea or topic. This topic must be supported with details. Cross out the detail that doesn't belong in each paragraph. Then write a new supporting detail below.

Monarchs are one of the most beautiful insects in the world. However, their bright colors aren't just for show. These colors warn birds that monarchs aren't very good to eat. Unfortunately, monarch butterflies are in danger of extinction. You can plant a butterfly garden. In some places, if you harm one of these pretty butterflies, you can receive a $500 fine!

_____

I love the snow. I love the cold, crisp feeling beneath my feet. I love to make snowmen in my front yard. I wish I had a new sled. And more than anything, I love a good snowball fight! Maybe that's why winter is my favorite season of the year.

_____

The Writing Process

As you complete the following writing activities, use this chart to help your writing be the best it can be!

Proofreading Marks

When checking your writing,
use these symbols to edit your work.

Proofreading Mark	Example
Take out a word.	My brother is ~~is~~ ten years old.
Add a comma.	I ate a sandwich, a yogurt, and an apple.
Put in a word.	sad I was very when I lost the contest.
Add a period.	I will be back soon.
Capitalize a letter.	i am glad to see you!
Make a letter lowercase.	That book was Wonderful.
Add quotation marks.	Nice work, Mrs. Grant said.
Spell correctly.	The movie was scaree.

Writing Checklist

The next time you write a story, use this checklist
to make sure you've done your best work.

Title of the story:

☐ I used capital letters and periods.

☐ I used interesting words.

☐ I checked the spelling of words I wasn't sure about.

☐ I practiced reading my story.

☐ I used my best handwriting.

Eraser

Silly Sentences

What kinds of sentences can you make out of your name? Write your name on the lines below. Then write as many silly sentences as you can using the letters to begin the words. For example, using the name **Thomas,** you might make this sentence: **Two happy otters made apple sodas**.

You may want to keep a thesaurus or dictionary on hand to help you find and spell fun words!

Your Name: _Bryant_ _____

1. _____

2. _____

3. _____

4. _____

5. _____

6. _____

7. _____

Number Sets

Think of things that come in sets, such as **two eyes**, **three wishes**, or **four wheels**. Write your ideas on the lines below. Make a poster about one number set. Write your ideas on the poster, and then illustrate or glue magazine pictures next to each one.

Things that come in twos:

_____   _____   _____

_____   _____   _____

Things that come in threes:

_____   _____   _____

_____   _____   _____

Things that come in fours:

_____   _____   _____

_____   _____   _____

Can you think of more things that come in number sets, such as tens or dozens?

Things that come in _____:

_____   _____   _____

_____   _____   _____

Tricky Titles

Think of names of familiar stories, such as *Little Red Riding Hood*. What are some other titles that might work for that story? Think of a new title for each story below. Be creative!

The Three Little Pigs

_____

Jack and the Beanstalk

_____

Cinderella

_____

The Wizard of Oz

_____

The Little Engine That Could

_____

Robin Hood

_____

Beauty and the Beast

_____

Charlotte's Web

_____

The Tortoise and the Hare

_____

If I Were President . . .

You've just been elected as President of the United States! You are a very powerful person and you can help people. Answer the questions below to tell what you would do while in the White House.

1. What is the first thing you would do?

    _____

    _____

    _____

2. What countries would you visit?

    _____

    _____

    _____

4. What would you do to help the poor and homeless?

    _____

    _____

    _____

5. What would you do about pollution?

    _____

    _____

    _____

Symbols of Freedom

In 1886, France gave the Statue of Liberty to the United States as a sign of international friendship and freedom. Write five things that this statue means to you and your family.

1. _____
   _____
   _____

2. _____
   _____
   _____

3. _____
   _____
   _____

4. _____
   _____
   _____

5. _____
   _____

Under the Bed

Imagine your surprise one day when you look under your bed and find a . . . ! What would you like to find under your bed? What would you NOT like to find under your bed? Write about your ideas below.

I would like to find a _____.

I would like to find this because _____

_____

_____

_____

I would not like to find a _____.

I would not like to find this because _____

_____

_____

_____

What If . . .

Write a response to one of these questions. Use your imagination!

What if . . .

. . . a Martian landed in your backyard?

. . . you had superhuman strength?

. . . money grew on trees?

_____

_____

_____

_____

_____

_____

_____

On another piece of paper, draw a picture to go with your story.

What If . . .

Write a response to one of these questions. Be creative!

What if . . .

. . . you were 40 feet tall?

. . . clouds were made of cotton candy?

. . . you met a magic dragon?

_____

_____

_____

_____

_____

_____

_____

On another piece of paper, draw a picture to go with your story.

A New Flag

You have been hired to design a new flag for the United States. The existing flag has 13 red and white stripes that stand for the original 13 colonies. The 50 stars stand for the 50 states.

Think of other symbols for the United States. Then draw your new flag design below. On the lines, explain what your symbols mean and why you decided on your design.

_____

_____

_____

_____

_____

_____

The Interview

If you could interview any famous person in history, who would it be? It could be a famous artist, musician, athlete, inventor, president, or other important person. What would you like to ask him or her?

Do a little research and
answer the questions below.

Name of famous person:

_____

Where was this person born?

_____

Where did he or she go to school?

_____

What is the person best known for?

_____

_____

What is this person most proud of?

_____

_____

Who had the biggest effect on this person's life?

_____

_____

Now, on another piece of paper, write an article about your famous person. Use your research to create your article.

Mystery Animal

Use the secret code to find "fun facts" about a mystery animal. To solve the code, write the letter of the alphabet that comes before each letter listed under the lines.

a b c d e f g h i j k l m
n o p q r s t u v w x y z

1. A group of these animals is called a $\underset{n}{M}$ $\underset{p}{0}$ $\underset{c}{b}$.

2. The babies of these animals are called $\underset{k}{j}$ $\underset{p}{0}$ $\underset{f}{e}$ $\underset{z}{y}$ $\underset{t}{s}$.

3. A baby lives in its mother's $\underset{q}{P}$ $\underset{p}{0}$ $\underset{v}{u}$ $\underset{d}{c}$ $\underset{i}{h}$ for ten months.

4. These animals have powerful $\underset{i}{h}$ $\underset{j}{i}$ $\underset{o}{n}$ $\underset{e}{d}$ $\underset{m}{l}$ $\underset{f}{e}$ $\underset{h}{g}$ $\underset{t}{s}$.

5. This animal can make a single $\underset{k}{j}$ $\underset{v}{u}$ $\underset{n}{m}$ $\underset{q}{p}$ as long as a school bus!

6. These animals live in $\underset{b}{a}$ $\underset{v}{u}$ $\underset{t}{s}$ $\underset{u}{t}$ $\underset{s}{r}$ $\underset{b}{a}$ $\underset{m}{l}$ $\underset{j}{i}$ $\underset{b}{a}$.

7. What is the name of this mystery animal?

$\underset{l}{K}$ $\underset{b}{a}$ $\underset{o}{n}$ $\underset{h}{g}$ $\underset{b}{a}$ $\underset{s}{r}$ $\underset{p}{0}$ $\underset{p}{0}$

Using the "fun facts" above, write a paragraph about the mystery animal on another piece of paper. If you like, do some research to find out more fun facts to include!

Fact vs. Opinion

Facts are true and can be proven. **Opinions** are what someone feels or thinks. Read the following story. Underline the facts. Then answer the questions below.

Jackie Robinson is the greatest baseball player of all time. He is an important figure in history because he was the first African American to play on a professional baseball team. Robinson was born in Cairo, Georgia in 1919. He went on to college at UCLA, a great university. He is best known for playing with the Brooklyn Dodgers, where he won the National League's Most Valuable Player award in 1949. Though he dealt with many hardships and prejudice, he remains the best player in history. To cap off his career, he was asked to join the Baseball Hall of Fame in 1962. There will never be another player like Jackie Robinson.

Write two opinions you found in the paragraph.

_____

_____

How do you know these are opinions?

_____

_____

How do you know the facts you underlined are facts?

_____

_____

Voice Your Opinion

Remember, an **opinion** is what someone thinks or feels. Write an opinion paragraph about something that is important or interesting to you. Include your thoughts and feelings about this topic. Support your topic with examples and reasons. Use a topic listed below, or think of one of your own.

Possible Topics	
• The best pet	• My most interesting relative
• My favorite movie or book	• My favorite subject in school
• My favorite sport	

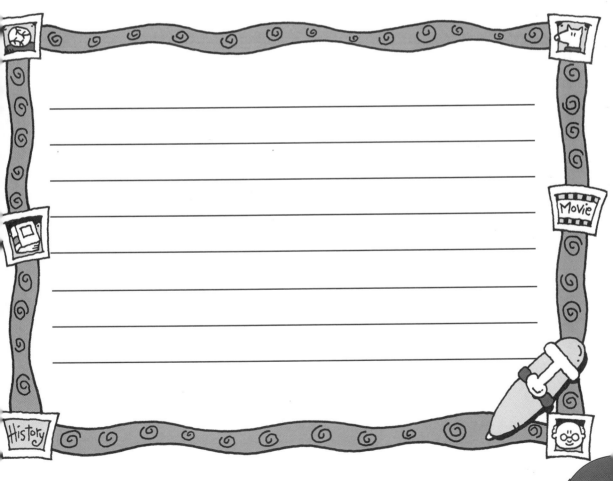

Super Similes

A **simile** is a comparison between two unlike objects, using the words **like** or **as**. For example: **He was as fast as lightning**. Use your imagination to complete these similes. Then illustrate one of your ideas in the box.

The kitten was as soft as _____.

He laughed like a _____.

My grandma is as sweet as _____.

Write your own simile on the line below.

_____

Making Metaphors

A **metaphor** is a comparison between two unlike objects, without using the words **like** or **as**. For example: **She is a delicate flower**. Use your imagination to complete these metaphors. Then illustrate one of your ideas in the box.

Mom is a gentle _____when tending her garden.

Dad is a growling _____in the morning.

Tyrell was a _____as he gobbled down the food.

Write your own metaphor on the line below.

_____

Amazing Analogies

An **analogy** is a comparison between two things that are somehow related.
For example: **Driver is to car as pilot is to plane.**

Complete these analogies.

1. Sun is to day as moon is to _____.

2. Cat is to kitten as horse is to _____.

3. Mom is to daughter as dad is to _____.

4. Teacher is to school as doctor is to _____.

5. Red is to apple as _____.

6. Thanksgiving is to fall as _____.

7. Bat is to baseball as _____.

Now, write two of your own analogies below.

_____

_____

Story Order

Stories are told in an order so they make sense to the reader. Put the sentences in the correct order to tell a story. Number the sentences from 1 to 5.

Hint: Look for words like **then, next, first, second, last,** and **finally.**

_____5_____ By the end of the day, he could ski down the hill without falling.

_____2_____ At first, he fell down a lot.

_____1_____ Last winter, Darius went skiing for the first time.

_____3_____ Then he took a ski lesson.

_____4_____ Darius practiced what he learned all afternoon.

More Story Order

Stories are told in an order so they make sense to the reader. Put the sentences in the correct order to tell a story. Number the sentences from 1 to 5.

_2_   Kitty didn't come when I called.

_1_   I woke up this morning and called for Kitty.

_3_   I put out her favorite food to see if she would come.

_5_   Finally, I found her. She was under the bed!

_4_   Then I checked all her favorite hiding places.

Giving Directions

Order is especially important when giving directions. For example, if a recipe's directions are out of order, the final product probably won't turn out right! Number the directions for this chocolate chip cookie recipe in order.

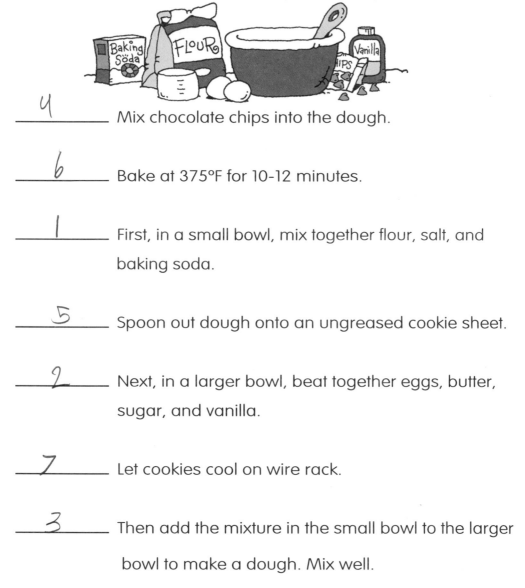

_____4_____ Mix chocolate chips into the dough.

_____6_____ Bake at 375°F for 10-12 minutes.

_____1_____ First, in a small bowl, mix together flour, salt, and baking soda.

_____5_____ Spoon out dough onto an ungreased cookie sheet.

_____2_____ Next, in a larger bowl, beat together eggs, butter, sugar, and vanilla.

_____7_____ Let cookies cool on wire rack.

_____3_____ Then add the mixture in the small bowl to the larger bowl to make a dough. Mix well.

Now, think of a simple food you know how to make, such as a peanut butter sandwich. Write your recipe on another piece of paper. Make sure to write the steps in the correct order.

This Is How You Do It!

What kinds of things do you do well? Can you cook a special meal? Can you construct a model airplane? Can you build a sand castle? Can you do a special dance or play a sport?

In the chart below, write out how to do an activity you do well. Begin with a simple introduction, and then write each step in order. Write a brief conclusion at the end.

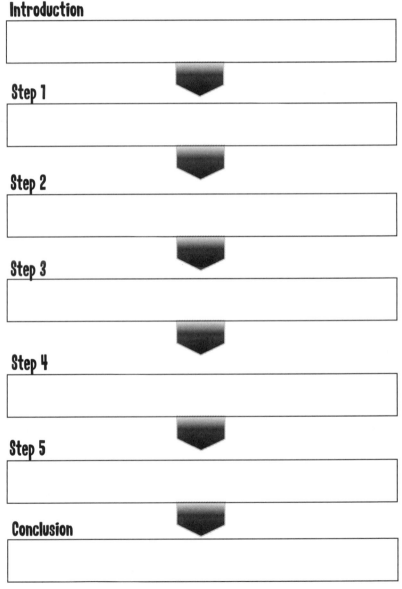

Introduction

Step 1

Step 2

Step 3

Step 4

Step 5

Conclusion

Picture Clues

Look carefully at each picture. Write who the person is, and then describe some clues in the picture that made you draw this conclusion. Next, write a sentence describing what is happening in the picture.

Person: _____

Clues: _____

Description: _____

_____

_____

_____

_____

Person: _____

Clues: _____

Description: _____

_____

_____

_____

What's Happening?

Look at the picture below. Make sure to notice all the details. Then use your imagination to write a story about it.

The Good Old Days

Talk with an older relative or friend about what it was like to live 30 or 40 years ago. Talk about music, clothes, popular games and sports, movies, and more! Then use the chart below to write information comparing the past to today.

THE PAST	TODAY

Now, on a separate piece of paper, write a paragraph or two comparing the past to today. Answer one of these questions:

I'm glad I didn't live in the past because . . .

I wish I had lived in the past because . . .

Learn Braille

Braille helps blind people to read. Real Braille uses raised dots that people can feel with their fingers. Use the braille symbols below to write your name.

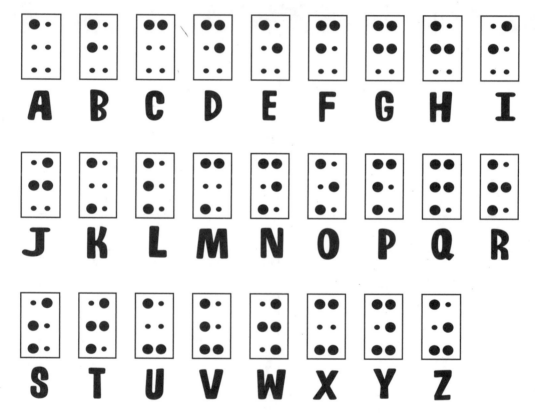

A B C D E F G H I

J K L M N O P Q R

S T U V W X Y Z

Write your name in Braille on the line below:

_____

Send Braille Mail!

Use the Braille symbols on page 50 to solve the puzzle below. Write a letter on each line.

W R I t i n g

i s   L o t s

o f   f u n !

Now, write your own Braille Mail for a friend or family member to solve!

In the News

Look through a local newspaper and read a couple of short articles. Notice that each article has a headline that grabs your attention. It should also include information that answers the following questions:

Who? What? When? Where? Why? How?

On the newspaper below, write an article about a recent event or activity with your family, at school, or with friends. Draw a picture to go with your article. Before writing your article, answer the questions below:

Who? _____   Where? _____

What? _____   Why? _____

When? _____   How? _____

Movie Report

Think of a movie you really love or one you don't like very much. Think of all the reasons you liked or disliked this movie. Then write a report about it on the lines below.

Movie title:

_____

Main characters:

_____

This is a _____ movie because _____

_____

The movie began with _____

_____

My favorite part was _____

_____

The most exciting part was _____

_____

The main characters learned to/changed by _____

_____

The movie ended with _____

_____

Edit a Narrative

A **narrative** is a story that describes something that happened to the writer. Read the following narrative. It has many mistakes. Use the proofreading marks on page 23 to make your corrections. Then rewrite the narrative correctly on another piece of paper.

My Grandmother

What can I say about my grandmother? she is won of the most interesting peeple I have ever known. Not only did she dance and sing in in the Theater, but she also wrote plays stories poetry, and was a great Artist. i am amazed by all the kreative things she could but theese are not the things that made her special to me.

My Grandmother was spesial because loved she me so much She went out of her way to to make every day fun and exciting! When I spent the night, she stayed up late telling me scarey stories. then she held my tiny hand all night as I slept And in the morning, eggs toast, and fruit were served on on her best Plates, and juice in her best crystal Wine glasses. these are only a few thing that my grandmother special two me.

My Narrative

Now that you know about narratives, choose a special person or event in your own life to write about. Answer the following questions, and then write your narrative on the lines below. Use extra paper if you need it.

What event or person will you write about?

_____

Why did you choose this event or person?

_____

_____

Write your narrative here:

_____

_____

_____

_____

_____

_____

_____

_____

Fairy Tale

A **fairy tale** is a make-believe story that usually includes many of these things:

- talking animals or objects
- castles and kingdoms
- royalty
- villains
- fairies, goblins, or dragons
- magic
- tricks, spells, or disguises
- a happy ending

Think about which of these things you'd like to include in your own fairy tale. You can make it as fantastic, magical, and silly as you wish! Write your fairy tale in the castle below. Use extra paper if you need it!

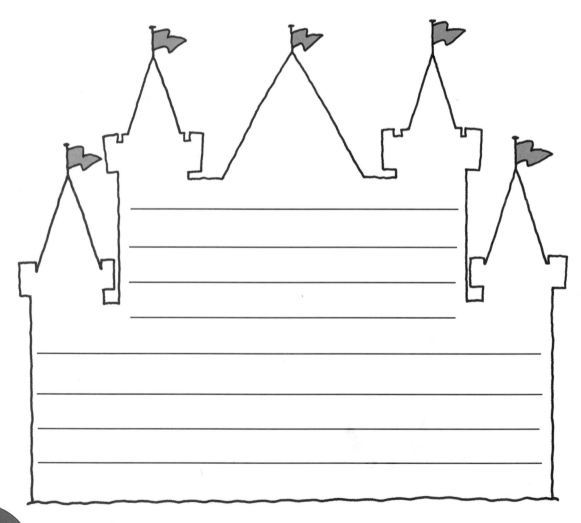

Write a Cinquain

A **cinquain** is a five-line poem that has a specific number of words or syllables.

Line 1: The subject—one word or two syllables

Line 2: Adjectives—two words or four syllables

Line 3: Action verbs—three words or six syllables

Line 4: Describing words—four to five words or eight syllables

Line 5: A word that sums up the subject—one word or two syllables

For example:

Rain

Soft, wet

Drizzling, pouring, misting

Kissing all the leaves and flowers

Droplets

Now, write your own cinquain! Follow the pattern above, and add illustrations around your poem.

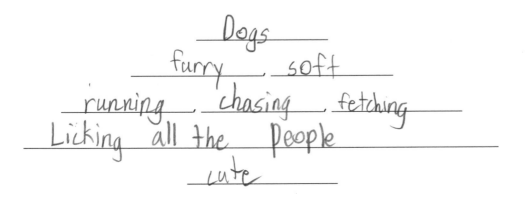

Dogs

furry, soft

running, chasing, fetching

Licking all the people

cute

Mysterious Myths

A **myth** is a make-believe story that explains how something "came to be." It usually tells about animals and other things in nature.

Think of a fun, imaginative myth you can make up about one of these topics:

- Why the sky is blue
- Where stars come from
- Why zebras have stripes
- Why dogs bark
- Why there are waves in the ocean
- Why cats sleep so much
- Why frogs can jump
- Why rain turns to snow

It's Me, Baby!

Ask one of your parents or caregivers what you were like as a baby. Then complete the worksheet below. Make sure to include lots of details. On another piece of paper, draw a a picture of yourself as a baby.

Name:_____ Birth date: _____

Birth weight:_____ Eye color:_____

Hair color:_____ My first word was _____.

I was _____ years old when I got my first tooth.

I was _____ years old when I took my first step.

My favorite toys were _____

_____

My favorite foods were _____

_____

My favorite games were_____

_____

I was a very special baby because _____

_____

_____

Recipe for a Best Friend

Fill out this recipe card for what you should "mix together" to make a best friend. First, think about all the qualities that make a good friend, and list them on another piece of paper. Then write out the qualities, recipe-style!

For example: 1. Start with one invitation to go bike riding.

2. Then toss in a pinch of smiles and laughs.

3. Mix it all together for a lot of fun!

My Heroes!

Heroes are people we look up to and respect. They are people we would like to model ourselves after and maybe be like when we grow up. You can find heroes in many different places. Write about your heroes below by completing these sentences.

1. My real-life hero is _____.

   This person is my hero because _____

   _____

   _____

2. Another real-life hero is _____.

   This person is my hero because _____

   _____

   _____

3. My movie hero is _____.

   This person is my hero because _____

   _____

   _____

4. My book hero is _____.

   This person is my hero because _____

   _____

   _____

On another piece of paper, write a letter to your hero. Explain why you have chosen this person as your hero.

Answer Key

Page 4
1. feel
2. sound
3. look
4. smell
5. taste
6. taste
7. feel
8. sound

Page 5
Answers will vary.

Page 6
1. creep
2. bounce
3. tumble
4. slouch
5. squint
6. grasp
7. prowl
8. strut

Page 7
1. hopeful
2. shocked
3. proud
4. doubtful
5. lonely
6. bored

Page 8-9
Answers will vary.

Page 10
Jamie woke up and **grinned**. Today was his birthday! He **bounced** out of bed and **raced** to the kitchen. His mom was baking him a **delicious** chocolate cake. "You better get ready," Mom said. "Your party **begins** in one hour." "I can't wait!" Jamie **shouted excitedly**. He **gobbled** his breakfast **quickly**, and then went to get dressed in his **finest** clothes. Little did Jamie know the special **present** that was waiting for him. He was **astonished**!

Page 11
1. meet
2. pair
3. scent
4. blew
5. mail
6. tale

Page 12
Answers will vary.

Page 13
Answers will vary.

Page 14
1. bite
2. mail
3. mend
4. sink
5. light
6. friend
7. whale
8. pink

Page 15
1. trail
2. squeak
3. sneeze
4. French fries

Page 16
1. bare chair
2. power flower
3. sad dad
4. ship trip
5. cute loot
6. sweet street
7. best nest

Page 17
1. I; answers will vary.
2. I; answers will vary.
3. C
4. I; answers will vary.
5. C
6. C
7. I; answers will vary.
8. I; answers will vary.

Page 18
We have been best friends for five years.

Brenda is better at math than reading.

We can't meet you tonight because we have too much homework.

Molly's new bike is shiny and red.

Ms. Gonzales was upset about her lost dog.

It isn't windy enough to fly a kite.

Caitlyn is the best swimmer on the swim team.

Page 19
Answers will vary.

Page 20
Answers will vary.

Page 21
Answers will vary.

Page 22
Answers will vary.

Page 23
"You can plant a butterfly garden" is crossed out; answers will vary.
"I wish I had a new sled" is crossed out; answers will vary.

Page 27
Answers will vary.

Page 28
Answers will vary.

Page 29
Answers will vary.

Page 30
Answers will vary.

Page 31
Answers will vary.

Page 32
Answers will vary.

Page 33
Answers will vary.

Page 34
Answers will vary.

Page 35
Answers will vary.

Answer Key

Page 36

Answers will vary.

Page 37

1. mob
2. joeys
3. pouch
4. hind legs
5. jump
6. Australia
7. kangaroo

Page 38

Answers will vary.

Page 39

Answers will vary.

Page 40

Answers will vary.

Page 41

Answers will vary.

Page 42

1. night
2. foal / pony
3. son
4. hospital
5. answers will vary
6. answers will vary
7. answers will vary

Page 43

5 By the end of the day, he could ski down the hill without falling.

2 At first, he fell down a lot.

1 Last winter, Darius went skiing for the first time.

3 Then he took a ski lesson.

4 Darius practiced what he learned all afternoon.

Page 44

2 Kitty didn't come when I called.

1 I woke up this morning and called for Kitty.

3 I put out her favorite food to see if she would come.

5 Finally, I found her. She was under the bed!

4 Then I checked all her favorite hiding places.

Page 45

4 Mix chocolate chips into the dough.

6 Bake at 375°F for 10-12 minutes.

1 First, in a small bowl, mix together flour, salt, and baking soda.

5 Spoon out dough onto an ungreased cookie sheet.

2 Next, in a larger bowl, beat together eggs, butter, sugar, and vanilla.

7 Let cookies cool on wire rack.

3 Then add the mixture in the small bowl to the larger bowl to make a dough. Mix well.

Page 46–53

Answers will vary.

Page 54

What can I say about my grandmother? she is won of the most interesting peeple I have ever known. Not only did she dance and sing in in the Theater, but she also wrote plays, stories, poetry, and was a great Artist. i am amazed by all the kreative things she could do but theese are not the things that made her special to me.

My Grandmother was spesial because loved she me so much. She went out of her way to to make every day fun and exciting! When I spent the night, she stayed up late telling me scarey stories. then she held my tiny hand all night as I slept. And in the morning, eggs, toast, and fruit were served on on her best Plates, and juice in her best crystal Wine glasses. these are only a few thing that my grandmother special two me.

Page 55-61

Answers will vary.

Eraser

SUPER!

Squeak